P9-BBU-574

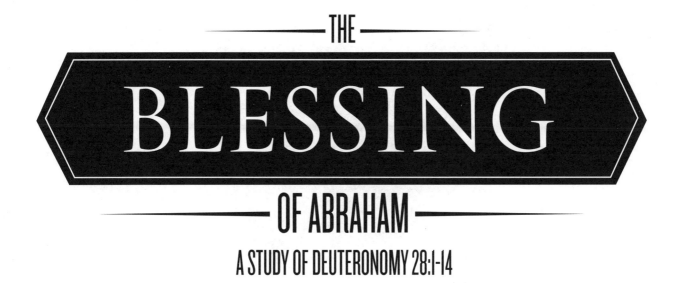

THE
BLESSING
OF ABRAHAM
A STUDY OF DEUTERONOMY 28:1-14

GLORIA COPELAND & PASTOR GEORGE PEARSONS

© 2014 Eagle Mountain International Church Inc. aka Kenneth Copeland Ministries. All rights reserved.
No part of this book may be reproduced or transmitted in any form or by any means, electronic or mechanical, including photocopying, recording, or by any information storage and retrieval system, without the written permission of the publisher.

For more information about Kenneth Copeland Ministries, visit kcm.org or call
1-800-600-7395 (U.S. only) or +1-817-852-6000.

ISBN 978-1-57562-622-2
#30-0832

Unless otherwise noted, all scripture is from the *King James Version* of the Bible.

Scripture quotations marked AMP are from *The Amplified Bible, Old Testament* © 1965, 1987 by the Zondervan Corporation. *The Amplified New Testament* © 1958, 1987 by The Lockman Foundation. Used by permission.

Scripture quotations marked NIV and NIV-84 are from *The Holy Bible, New International Version* © 1973, 1978, 1984, 2011 by Biblica Inc. Used by permission. All rights reserved worldwide.

Scripture quotations marked MSG are from *The Message* © 1993, 1994, 1995, 1996, 2000, 2001, 2002. Used by permission of NavPress Publishing Group.

Scripture quotations marked NLT and NLT-96 are from the *Holy Bible, New Living Translation* © 1996, 2004 by Tyndale Charitable Trust. Used by permission of Tyndale House Publishers.

Scripture quotations marked NKJV are from the *New King James Version* © 1982 by Thomas Nelson Inc.

Scripture quotations marked ESV are from *The Holy Bible, English Standard Version*® © 2001 by Crossway, a publishing ministry of Good News Publishers. Used by permission. All rights reserved.

Scripture quotations marked CEV are from the *Contemporary English Version* © 1991, 1992, 1995 by American Bible Society. Used by permission.

Scripture quotations marked BBE are from the *Bible in Basic English,* public domain.

Scripture quotations marked CEB are from the *Common English Bible*® © 2012 Common English Bible. All rights reserved.

Scripture quotations marked *Brenton* are from English Translation of the Greek Septuagint Bible, The Translation of the Greek Old Testament Scriptures With Apocrypha; Compiled from the Translation by Sir Lancelot C.L. Brenton (Samuel Bagster and Sons, Ltd., 1851), public domain.

Scripture quotations marked VOICE are from *The Voice Bible* © 2012 Thomas Nelson Inc. All rights reserved.

Scripture quotations marked EXB are from *The Expanded Bible* © 2011 Thomas Nelson Inc. Used by permission. All rights reserved.

Quotations from *John Gill's Expositions of the Bible,* a work originally published in two parts: *An Exposition of the New Testament* (1746-8), and *An Exposition of the Old Testament* (1748-63), public domain.

Quotations from *Adam Clarke's Commentary on the Bible, Abridged by Ralph Earle* (World Bible Publishers Inc., Iowa Falls, Iowa, originally published by Baker Books, a division of Baker Book House Company, Grand Rapids, Mich., © 1967 Beacon Hill Press of Kansas City), page 224.

Day 1
Quote from Gloria Copeland, *50 Days of Prosperity Vol. 2* (Fort Worth, Kenneth Copeland Publications), Day #100.
"A Bitter Pill to Swallow" excerpt from Kenneth Copeland, *THE BLESSING of The LORD Makes Rich and He Adds No Sorrow With It Proverbs 10:22* (Fort Worth: Kenneth Copeland Publications, 2011), pages 82-83.

Day 2
Quotation from *The Chumash, The Gutnick Edition,* Rabbi Chaim Miller, *The Gutnick Edition Chumash,* Synagogue Edition, © 2003-9 by Chaim Miller (Kol Menachem, Brooklyn, New York), page 1305.
"Clearing Up the Confusion" excerpt from Kenneth Copeland, *THE BLESSING of The LORD Makes Rich and He Adds No Sorrow With It Proverbs 10:22* (Fort Worth: Kenneth Copeland Publications, 2011), pages 134-135.

"Who Taught These Guys How to Fight?" excerpt from Kenneth Copeland, *THE BLESSING of The LORD Makes Rich and He Adds No Sorrow With It Proverbs 10:22* (Fort Worth: Kenneth Copeland Publications, 2011), pages 99-100.

Days 2, 4
1. "Why Do Jews Win So Many Nobels?" by Ruth Schuster, as posted online by Haaretz.com, http://www.haaretz.com/jewish-world/jewish-world-news/1.551520 (accessed April 29, 2014).
2. "Facts About Israel," as posted online by Israel21C, http://israel21c.org/did-you-know-israel-facts (accessed April 29, 2014).
3. "65 Years of Innovation, From Rummikub to the 'God Particle'" by Marcella Rosen, as posted online by The Times of Israel, http://www.timesofisrael.com/65-years-of-innovation-from-rummikub-to-the-god-particle (accessed April 29, 2014).
4. "Some of Israel's Accomplishments," as posted online by FactsandLogic.org, http://www.factsandlogic.org/outstanding_accomp_pr.html (accessed April 29, 2014).
5. "Israelis Develop West Nile Vaccine," as posted online by Israel21C, http://israel21c.org/health/israelis-develop-west-nile-vaccine (accessed April 29, 2014).

Days 3, 5, 6, 7, 10
Quotation from *The Chumash, Stone Edition,* Rabbi Nosson Scherman, *The Chumash, Vol. 1:* Bereishis/Genesis, Personal Size Edition, Artscroll Series, Stone Edition (New York: Mesorah Publications Ltd.), pages 1076-1077, and (Day 10) 1016.

Day 6, 8, 10
Quotation from *Commentary on the Old Testament in Ten Volumes, Volume 1, The Pentateuch* by C.F. Keil and F. Delitzsch, translated from the German by James Martin (William B. Berdmans Publishing Co., Grand Rapids, Mich., 1986), pages 436-437.

Day 9
References to the "God's Great Storehouse" prophecy are taken from the "What About 2012" prophecy, © 2011 Kenneth Copeland. All rights reserved.
"Come to the Table" prophecy delivered by Kenneth Copeland on August 7, 2009, at 2009 Southwest Believers' Convention, Fort Worth, Texas.
"The Lord of the Storehouse" prophecy delivered by Kenneth Copeland on January 23, 2012.
"And I Will Bless You Beyond Your Means" prophecy delivered by Kenneth Copeland on July 9, 2007, at the 2007 West Coast Believers' Convention, Anaheim, Calif.

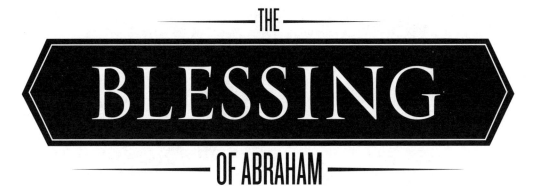

THE BLESSING OF ABRAHAM

GLORIA COPELAND & PASTOR GEORGE PEARSONS

TABLE OF CONTENTS

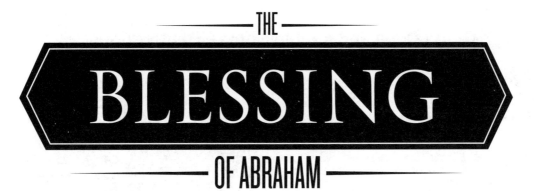

THE BLESSING OF ABRAHAM

GLORIA COPELAND & PASTOR GEORGE PEARSONS

DEUTERONOMY 28:1-14

1   And it shall come to pass, if thou shalt hearken diligently unto the voice of the Lord thy God, to observe and to do all his commandments which I command thee this day, that the Lord thy God will set thee on high above all nations of the earth:

2   And all these blessings shall come on thee, and overtake thee, if thou shalt hearken unto the voice of the Lord thy God.

3   Blessed shalt thou be in the city, and blessed shalt thou be in the field.

4   Blessed shall be the fruit of thy body, and the fruit of thy ground, and the fruit of thy cattle, the increase of thy kine, and the flocks of thy sheep.

5   Blessed shall be thy basket and thy store.

6   Blessed shalt thou be when thou comest in, and blessed shalt thou be when thou goest out.

7   The Lord shall cause thine enemies that rise up against thee to be smitten before thy face: they shall come out against thee one way, and flee before thee seven ways.

8   The Lord shall command the blessing upon thee in thy storehouses, and in all that thou settest thine hand unto; and he shall bless thee in the land which the Lord thy God giveth thee.

9   The Lord shall establish thee an holy people unto himself, as he hath sworn unto thee, if thou shalt keep the commandments of the Lord thy God, and walk in his ways.

10   And all people of the earth shall see that thou art called by the name of the Lord; and they shall be afraid of thee.

11   And the Lord shall make thee plenteous in goods, in the fruit of thy body, and in the fruit of thy cattle, and in the fruit of thy ground, in the land which the Lord sware unto thy fathers to give thee.

12   The Lord shall open unto thee his good treasure, the heaven to give the rain unto thy land in his season, and to bless all the work of thine hand: and thou shalt lend unto many nations, and thou shalt not borrow.

13   And the Lord shall make thee the head, and not the tail; and thou shalt be above only, and thou shalt not be beneath; if that thou hearken unto the commandments of the Lord thy God, which I command thee this day, to observe and to do them:

14   And thou shalt not go aside from any of the words which I command thee this day, to the right hand, or to the left, to go after other gods to serve them.

Handwritten top:
The Law of the Spirit of Life in Christ Jesus has made me free from the law of sin & death Ro 8:2

God's promise + oath to bless = Gen 22, 26

28:63 "the Lord rejoiced over them to do them good.

Blessing almost all holy prosperity that holy

Curses of the law. Blessings for obedience

15 ᵃCursed *be* the man that maketh *any* graven or molten image, an abomination unto the LORD, the work of the hands of the craftsman, and putteth *it* in *a* secret *place.* ᵉAnd all the people shall answer and say, Ä′-mĕn.

16 ᵉCursed *be* he that setteth light by his father or his mother. And all the people shall say, Ä′-mĕn.

17 ᶠCursed *be* he that removeth his neighbour's landmark. And all the people shall say, Ä′-mĕn.

18 ⁱCursed *be* he that maketh the blind to wander out of the way. And all the people shall say, Ä′-mĕn.

19 ʲCursed *be* he that perverteth the judgment of the stranger, fatherless, and widow. And all the people shall say, Ä′-mĕn.

20 ˡCursed *be* he that lieth with his father's wife; because he uncovereth his father's skirt. And all the people shall say, Ä′-mĕn.

21 ⁿCursed *be* he that lieth with any manner of beast. And all the people shall say, Ä′-mĕn.

22 ᵒCursed *be* he that lieth with his sister, the daughter of his father, or the daughter of his mother. And all the people shall say, Ä′-mĕn.

23 ᵖCursed *be* he that lieth with his mother in law. And all the people shall say, Ä′-mĕn.

24 ʳCursed *be* he that smiteth his neighbour secretly. And all the people shall say, Ä′-mĕn.

25 ˢCursed *be* he that taketh reward to slay an innocent person. And all the people shall say, Ä′-mĕn.

26 ᵘCursed *be* he that confirmeth not *all* the words of this law to do them. And all the people shall say, Ä′-mĕn.

condition = hearken

CHAPTER 28

IF! AND it shall come to pass, *if* thou shalt (hearken) diligently unto the voice of the make adjustments 267

LORD thy God, to observe and to do all his commandments which I command thee this day, that the LORD thy God will set thee on ᵇhigh above all nations of the earth:

2 And (all these blessings) shall come on thee, and ᵈovertake thee, if thou shalt hearken unto the voice of the LORD thy God.

3 ᵉBlessed *shalt* thou be in the city, and blessed *shalt* thou *be* ᵍin the field.

4 Blessed *shall be* ʰthe fruit of thy (body) and the fruit of thy ground, and the fruit of thy cattle, the (increase) of thy kine, and the flocks of thy sheep.

5 Blessed *shall be* thy basket and thy ¹store.

6 Blessed *shalt* thou *be* ᵏwhen thou comest in, and blessed *shalt* thou *be* when thou goest out.

7 The LORD ᵐshall cause thine enemies that rise up against thee to be smitten before thy face: they shall come out against thee one way, and flee before thee seven ways.

8 The LORD shall command the blessing upon thee in thy ²storehouses, and in all that thou settest thine hand unto; and he shall bless thee in the land which the LORD thy God giveth thee.

9 ᵍThe LORD shall establish thee an holy people unto himself, as he hath sworn unto thee, (if) thou shalt keep the commandments of the LORD thy God, and walk in his ways.

10 And all people of the earth shall (see) that thou art ᵗcalled by the name of the LORD; and they shall be ᵛafraid of thee.

11 And the LORD shall make thee plenteous ³in goods, in the fruit of thy (body) and in the fruit of thy cattle, and in the fruit of thy ground, in the land which the LORD sware unto thy fathers to give thee.

12 The LORD shall open unto

Center margin refs: a Ex. 20.4 & 34.17. So Isa. 44.9. Hos. 13.2. b ch. 26.19. c Cp. Nu. 5.22. Jer. 11.5. 1 Co. 14.16. d Zech. 1.6. e So Ex. 20.12 & 21.17. Lev. 19.3. ch. 21.13-21. f ch. 19.14. g Ge. 39.5. h Ge. 49.25. ch. 7.13. 1 Tim. 4.8. i Lev. 19.14. j ch. 24.17. 1 Or, *dough, or, kneading trough.* k Ps. 121.8. l Lev. 18.8. m 2 Sa. 22.38-41. Ps. 18.37-40. David Ps 89.20-36 n Lev. 18.23. o Lev. 18.9 & 20.17. 2 Or, *barns.* Ps133:3 p Lev. 18.17 & 20.14. q Ex. 19.5. ch. 7.6. r Ex. 21.12, 14. ch. 19.11. s Ex. 23.7, 8. Ezek. 22.12. Nu. 6.27. u Jer. 11.3. Gal. 3.10. ch. 11.25. 3 Or, *for good.* 4 Heb. *belly.*

Right margin handwritten:
SHALOM = WHOLE
29:9 hearken + do
2-13 = all blessings
high place Surely goodness + mercy overtakes me
Serve God and use money - not serve money & use God.
overtaken with blessings!
Body - Soul - Spirit = you
prosperity offspring
Barren is a curse! Deut 7:14
your prosperity is in the blessings.
coming + going
Debt + lack = greatest enemies
enemies defeated = continual victory
20:1-4 Is 54:17 Ps
Blessing on Storehouse Jer 7:23
everything you do!
give you the land Deut 8:18
HOLY PEOPLE = Blessed people 9-13
Ex 19:5 Mal 2:1,5 Ps 112:10
Jos 2:9-11 Deut 7:12-15
you shall be a testimony Ps 126:1-3
Deut 11:25 Ps 112:9-10
Deut 2:24-25
plenty of everything
v.10 v.45-47
Is 61:9 - all shall acknowledge
VII "surplus of pros."
The Lord's treasure open to you
with all
Prosperity
Your blessing is a sign
The curse is also a sign 45-46
forfeit blessing by rejecting wisdom Prov 9:12

Bottom handwritten:
Prosperity a command v.1 29:9 hearken +
28:63: prosper
Prv 1:32 Prosperity destroys the fool
Job 36:11-12
This is a perfect law of liberty
Lev 18:24 (Sexual sins) defile land "from the beginning earth has shared consequences of mans guilt. B. See note 154 p.

V10 Bless = Arw 1-6
We have been blessed with spiritual blessing. Eph
v.10 See your blessing. Your blessing is a sign
M 169 forfeit blessing by rejecting wisdom Prov 9:12

iniquities turn away blessings & keep good from you. Jer 5: 23-26
Eye for an eye 4 days ⃝ *There was no curse before Adam sinned.*
There was no poverty before Adam sinned.

DEUTERONOMY 28 *(Rain) Ps 146:8, 147:18* *Ps 69:10* *Zech short* *The curses for disobedience*

How much is left after "all"

thee his good treasure, the heaven ᵃto give the rain unto thy land in his season, and to bless all the work of thine hand: and ᶜthou shalt lend unto many nations, and thou shalt not borrow. v.44 *Deut 15:6*

work blessed
no debt $

(13) And the LORD shall make thee ᵉthe head, and not the tail; and thou shalt be above only, and thou shalt not be beneath; if that thou hearken unto the commandments of the LORD thy God, which I command thee this day, to observe and to do them: *hearken = ✓*

above - head
Is 2:6 agreements with outsiders
if! observe & do! who receives Blessing Ps 24:3-5

(14) ᵍAnd thou shalt not go aside from any of the words which I command thee this day, to the right hand, or to the left, to go after other gods to serve them.

only blessing for me I take no curse

15 ¶ But it shall come to pass, ⁱif thou wilt not hearken unto the voice of the LORD thy God, to observe to do all his commandments and his statutes which I command thee this day; that all these curses shall come upon thee, and overtake thee: *v.62*

curses shall curse come on you (you choose 30:19)

Leave your protection thru fear & curse is there. Fear connects to curse. faith delivers from curse

16 Cursed shalt thou be ᵐin the city, and cursed shalt thou be in the field.

curse = bitterness Gal 3:13 redeemed

17 Cursed shall be thy basket and thy store.

18 Cursed shall be the fruit of thy body, and the fruit of thy land, the increase of thy kine, and the flocks of thy sheep.

19 Cursed shalt thou be when thou comest in, and cursed shalt thou be when thou goest out.

NKJ "confusion"
Everything cursed Jer 17:3

20 The LORD ˢshall send upon thee cursing, vexation, and ᵗrebuke, in all that thou settest thine hand unto ³for to do, until thou be destroyed, and until thou perish quickly; because of the wickedness of thy doings, whereby thou hast forsaken me. v.15 (See NKJ)

Lord allows what you choose
perish because of the wickedness of your doings
Pestilence (plague)

21 The LORD shall make ʷthe pestilence cleave unto thee, until he have consumed thee

---

from off the land, whither thou goest to possess it. *will have to allow*

22 The LORD shall smite thee *you to be smitten* with ᵇa consumption, and with ᵇa fever, and with an inflammation, and with an extreme burning, and with the ¹sword, and with ᵈblasting, and with ᵈmildew; and they shall pursue thee until thou perish.

23 And ᶠthy heaven that is over thy head shall be brass, and the earth that is under thee shall be iron.

24 The LORD shall make the rain of thy land powder and dust: from heaven shall it come down upon thee, until thou be destroyed.

25 ʰThe LORD shall cause thee to be smitten before thine enemies: thou shalt go out one way against them, and flee seven ways before them: and ʲshalt be ²removed into all the kingdoms of the earth.

26 And ᵏthy carcase shall be meat unto all fowls of the air, and unto the beasts of the earth, and ˡno man shall fray them away. *tumors NLT Amp*

27 The LORD will smite thee with ⁿthe botch of Egypt, and with ᵒthe emerods, and with the scab, and with the itch, whereof thou canst not be healed.

28 The LORD shall smite thee with ᵖmadness, and blindness, and ᵠastonishment of heart:

(29) And thou shalt ʳgrope at noonday, as the blind gropeth in darkness, and thou shalt not prosper in thy ways: and thou shalt be only oppressed and spoiled evermore, and no man shall save thee. *Ripped off* *Health to mind to job a rip*

30 ᵘThou shalt betroth a wife, and another man shall lie with her: ᵛthou shalt build an house, and thou shalt not dwell therein: thou shalt plant a vineyard, and shalt not ⁴gather the grapes thereof. *Ps 128:2 3* *curse adult*

31 Thine ox shall be slain before thine eyes, and thou

Side column references:
a Lev. 26. 4.
ch. 11. 14.
b Lev. 26. 16.
c ch. 15. 6.
1 Or, drought.
d Am. 4. 9.
Hag. 2. 17.
e Isa. 9. 14, 15.
f Lev. 26. 19.
Prov 22:1 Rich will own poor
g ch. 5. 32. *hearkening diligently*
h Lev. 26. 17, 37. ch. 32. 30.
Is 34:5 B
i Lev. 26. 14. Lam. 2. 17. Dan. 9. 11, 13. Mal. 2. 2. Bar. 1. 20. Ezek. 23. 46.
2 Heb. for a removing.
k Ps. 79. 2. Jer. 7. 33 & 16. 4.
l Jer. 7. 33. m ver. 3-6. n ver. 35. o 1 Sa. 5. 6.
p Zech. 12. 4.
q Jer. 4. 9.
r Job 5. 14. Isa. 59. 10.
s Mal. 2. 2.
t Isa. 30. 17 & 51. 20 & 66. 15.
3 Heb. which thou wouldest do.
u ch. 20. 5-7. v Am. 5. 11. Zeph. 1. 13.
4 Heb. profane, or, use it as common meat.
w Lev. 26. 25.

268

Bottom handwritten notes:

V20 NKJ= "cursing confusion"
24:22
Curse is out there & working.
You have a choice
Young's "Hints to Bible interpretation"

Ps 115:14!
"These words provide a most accurate description of the true nature of "blessing." (Heb) Blessing means increase and abundance, whereas the closest definition of curse (Heb) is decrease & less." T 1381 & Ps 8:7 T

Man's corruption brought curses upon heaven & earth" T 1381
= curse is result of man's corruption

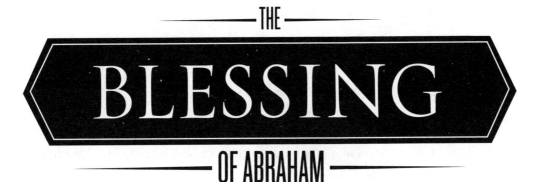

THE BLESSING OF ABRAHAM

GLORIA COPELAND & PASTOR GEORGE PEARSONS

REDEEMED FROM THE CURSE

DAY 1

A. Galatians 3:13—Redeemed From the Curse

1. AMP: "Christ purchased our freedom [redeeming us] from the curse (doom) of the Law [and its condemnation] by [Himself] becoming a curse for us."

2. The curse is a declaration which dooms someone to failure.

   a. To destroy, do away with, cease, terminate

   b. To render idle, unemployed, inactive

   c. To cause a person or thing to have no further efficiency

   d. To deprive of force, influence, power

   e. See "A Bitter Pill to Swallow," page 13

3. Everything that could go wrong, goes wrong.

4. The curse is found in Deuteronomy 28:15-68.

5. *Redeemed from the curse* (GK) = purchased, ransomed, paid for, rescued

6. Christ has purchased us, ransomed us and rescued us from the curse of doom, destruction and failure.

   a. 1 Corinthians 6:20 (NLT): "God bought you with a high price."

   b. 1 Peter 1:18-19 (NKJV): "Knowing that you were not redeemed with corruptible things...but with the precious blood of Christ, as of a lamb without blemish and without spot."

B. Galatians 3:14—THE BLESSING of Abraham

1. THE BLESSING is a declaration which empowers someone to succeed.

2. Genesis 1:28: "And God blessed them, and God said unto them, Be fruitful, multiply, and replenish the earth, and subdue it: and have dominion over...every living thing."

3. Proverbs 10:22 (AMP): "The blessing of the Lord—it makes [truly] rich, and He adds no sorrow with it [neither does toiling increase it]."

4. Everything that could go right, goes right.

5. Deuteronomy 8:18 (NLT): "Remember the Lord your God. He is the one who gives you power to be successful, in order to fulfill the covenant he confirmed to your ancestors with an oath."

6. THE BLESSING of Abraham is found in Deuteronomy 28:1-14.

C. Galatians 3:14—Blessed With Abraham

1. We are to receive by faith everything that the Spirit promised Abraham.

2. NLT: "Through Christ Jesus, God has blessed the Gentiles with the same blessing He promised to Abraham."

3. Verse 9 (ESV): "Those who are of faith are blessed along with Abraham, the man of faith."

4. Verse 29 (NKJV): "If you are Christ's, then you are Abraham's seed, and heirs according to the promise."

5. "Under the curse you diminish. Things flow away from you. Under THE BLESSING, you increase. Things flow into you." —Gloria Copeland, *50 Days of Prosperity Vol. 2*

A BITTER PILL TO SWALLOW

From *THE BLESSING of The LORD Makes Rich and He Adds No Sorrow With It*

— by Kenneth Copeland —

It's no wonder the Hebrew root of the word *curse* means "bitterness" because the curse made Adam and Eve's lives bitter in every way. It embittered both the spirit realm and the natural realm. It caused the animals Adam had named to see him as their enemy instead of their benefactor. Even the ground became bitter toward mankind. Instead

> "...the moment Adam and Eve's sin was revealed...He began revealing His merciful plan."

of joyfully producing abundant fruit for them to eat, it didn't want to grow anything. Adam, who had once lived in a marvelous, beautiful place filled with abundance, was forced to scratch a living out of ground that rebuked him every time he tried to plant it and harvest it. He had to sweat and strain (Hebrew: *toil*) to earn a living, knowing the whole time that God had not designed him to *earn* a living, but to *create* a living.

Every aspect of the curse came as a horrible shock to Adam and Eve. Nothing in them was created to deal with it. Their spirits weren't created to be infested with death and darkness. They were created to be filled with life and light. Their minds weren't made to house things like hatred and fear. They were made for love and faith. Their bodies were designed for health—not sickness and disease.

Death, in all its manifestation, is totally foreign to human beings. The curse is completely contrary to the way God made us. That's why the body fights those things. Our whole system rebels against them because they don't have any business in or on us. When sin, hate, fear and

> "God Himself would become Son of Man, bear the bitterness of the curse and forever restore THE BLESSING."

other aspects of the curse invade us, our bodies recognize them as opposing, alien forces and begin to fight them. The body will fight those things until it dies.

Adam must have panicked as the consequences of the curse began to dawn on him. He must have thought, *How am I ever going to get out of this? My seed is bitter, so even my children will be affected by it. The earth is bitter. The animal kingdom is bitter. I've even embittered my relationship with God. Oh, God, how can I ever be Your friend again?*

Before he could even ask those questions, however, they were answered. God answered them before the foundation of the world, when He foresaw that mankind would fall. So, the moment Adam and Eve's sin was revealed and they stood before God, stripped of their former glory, He began revealing His merciful plan. He spoke about the Seed of the woman who would one day crush the serpent's head. He pointed down through the corridor of time to the last Adam, the Redeemer, who would undo what Satan had done through the first Adam. He gave the first clues to the mystery that would be kept secret for thousands of years: that God Himself would become the Son of Man, bear the bitterness of the curse and forever restore THE BLESSING.

"...in His great mercy, God ensured that mankind would not live eternally in this fallen state."

Then, God did for His beloved Adam and Eve what had to be done. Sacrificing an animal, He covered their nakedness and shame by making them tunics of skin. Through that sacrifice, He established the first blood covenant. He atoned for their sin and made a way to retain some form of relationship with them. Then, in His great mercy, God ensured that mankind would not live eternally in this fallen state.

NOTES

NOTES

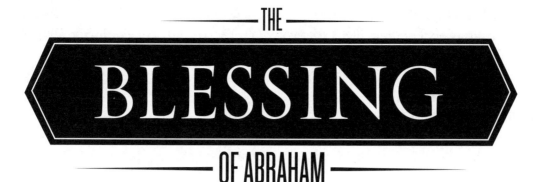

HIGH ABOVE ALL NATIONS (VERSE 1)

DAY 2

A. THE BLESSING Will Come to Pass...IF

1. There are conditions to THE BLESSING.

2. God is not trying to keep us from THE BLESSING—He is determined to see us walk in the fullness of THE BLESSING.

3. If you will listen diligently to the voice of the Lord your God

    a. Matthew 13:16: "Blessed are your eyes, for they see: and your ears, for they hear."

    b. John 10:27: "My sheep hear my voice, and I know them, and they follow me."

    c. Psalm 85:8: "I will hear what God the Lord will speak."

4. If you will observe His commandments

    a. God explained THE BLESSING in detail to the children of Israel—what it included and how it operated.

    b. He wanted to renew their minds from a bondage and lack mentality in Egypt to a BLESSING and prosperity mentality in Canaan.

    c. Why? So that THE BLESSING on them would create a Garden of Eden wherever they went.

    d. "Through Jesus, we get back in the Garden." —Gloria Copeland

    e. See "Clearing Up the Confusion," page 20

5. If you will do His commandments

    a. James 1:22-25 (NLT): "But don't just listen to God's word. You must do what it says. Otherwise, you are only fooling yourselves. For if you listen to the word and don't obey, it is like glancing at your face in a mirror. You see yourself, walk away, and forget what you look like. But if you look carefully into the perfect law that sets you free, and if you do what it says and don't forget what you heard, then God will bless you for doing it."

      b.   Joshua 1:8 (AMP): "This Book of the Law shall not depart out of your mouth, but you shall meditate on it day and night, that you may observe and do according to all that is written in it. For then you shall make your way prosperous, and then you shall deal wisely and have good success."

B. Set You on High Above the Nations

1. This is the first article of THE BLESSING of Abraham.

2. "God, your God, will make you an elite (nation), above all the nations of the earth." — *The Chumash, The Gutnick Edition,* page 1305

3. Proverbs 11:11 (NIV): "Through THE BLESSING of the upright a city is exalted, but by the mouth of the wicked it is destroyed."

4. Deuteronomy 28:7, 12 makes it clear that this includes military and economic supremacy over all other nations.
   a. Verse 7 (NLT): "The Lord will conquer your enemies when they attack you. They will attack you from one direction, but they will scatter from you in seven!"
   b. Verse 12 (NLT): "The Lord will send rain at the proper time from his rich treasury in the heavens and will bless all the work you do. You will lend to many nations, but you will never need to borrow from them."
   c. See "Who Taught These Guys How to Fight?" page 21

5. You will not be dominated or destroyed by other nations.

6. Twenty-two percent of Nobel Prize winners are Jewish.[1]

7. Jews make up only 0.2% of the world population.[1]

C. Set on High With Christ Jesus

1. Ephesians 2:6 (AMP): "And He raised us up together with Him and made us sit down together [giving us joint seating with Him] in the heavenly sphere [by virtue of our being] in Christ Jesus (the Messiah, the Anointed One)."

2. Ephesians 2:6 (MSG): "Then he picked us up and set us down in highest heaven in company with Jesus, our Messiah."

3. Colossians 1:13—We have been delivered from the power of darkness and have been translated into the kingdom of God.
   a. We have been set on high in dominion over powers and principalities.
   b. We rule over darkness.

c. "We have authority in the Name of Jesus, and we rule over darkness. But, *we* have to rule. If don't want the devil coming into our affairs, our bodies, our marriages, our finances, *we* have to say, 'You're not coming in here, Devil.' We have to stand our ground, and we have to say right words." —Gloria Copeland

4. Ephesians 6:10-14: "Finally, my brethren, be strong in the Lord, and in the power of his might. Put on the whole armour of God, that ye may be able to stand against the wiles of the devil. For we wrestle not against flesh and blood, but against principalities, against powers, against the rulers of the darkness of this world, against spiritual wickedness in high places. Wherefore take unto you the whole armour of God, that ye may be able to withstand in the evil day, and having done all, to stand. Stand therefore, having your loins girt about with truth, and having on the breastplate of righteousness."

CLEARING UP THE CONFUSION

From *THE BLESSING of The LORD Makes Rich and He Adds No Sorrow With It*

by Kenneth Copeland

This is why it was so important for God to get the commandments to the children of Israel. It explains why He went to such great lengths to describe to them in detail their covenant of BLESSING and how it operates.

He wanted to renew their minds because whatever they carried on the inside would eventually come out. If they carried a mindset of bondage, they'd turn even the Promised Land into a place of bondage. But if they carried within them the mindset of BLESSING, that BLESSING would create a Garden of Eden wherever they went.

The same thing is true for us as New Testament believers, but we have a major advantage. We have a regenerated spirit that's been made righteous. We have available to us the mind of Christ. We have the very image of Jesus inside us. God has "BLESSED us with all spiritual BLESSINGS in heavenly places in Christ."

> **"THE BLESSING will produce the conditions of the Garden of Eden around us as surely as it did for the Israelites in the Promised Land."**

If we'll just believe what the Bible says about us and walk in the covenant of love, THE BLESSING will produce the conditions of the Garden of Eden around us as surely as it did for the Israelites in the Promised Land. In fact, it will do even more for us than it did for them. Because we carry THE BLESSING inside us wherever we go, God can send us to the hardest, thistle-growing, demon-infested place, and we can go with joy. We don't have to argue with Him about it. We don't have to complain and drag our feet. We can go in faith knowing that God is sending us there not to live in squalor but to release THE BLESSING that's within us and turn that dark corner of the world into a milk-and-honey kind of place.

"Oh, Brother Copeland, you're not being practical. There are some places even THE BLESSING won't work."

If there are, I've never seen them, and I've been to a lot of places. I've seen THE BLESSING work everywhere from the wilds of Africa to the urban jungles of America.

WHO TAUGHT THESE GUYS HOW TO FIGHT?

From *THE BLESSING of The LORD Makes Rich and He Adds No Sorrow With It*

— by Kenneth Copeland —

When the battle was over, Abraham's household army had not only whipped the four-king, military machine that had conquered everyone in that part of the world; they had stripped them of all their spoils. "And he brought back all the goods, and also brought again his brother Lot, and his goods, and the women also, and the people" (Genesis 14 verse 16).

Talk about an upset! How on earth were Abraham and his servants able to pull off such an overwhelming victory? Where did they get the war technology to do that?

From THE BLESSING.

"Brother Copeland, surely you aren't saying that THE BLESSING taught them how to fight!"

That's exactly what I'm saying. What's more important, the Scriptures indicate the servants born in Abraham's house were trained warriors. Who trained them? Abraham couldn't have done it. He wasn't a military man. If a soldier or commander from another army had come in to train them, Abraham's servants wouldn't have had an edge on Ched's army at all. They would have been using the same battle strategies that he, and everyone else, was using. Clearly, someone taught Abraham's men military tactics no one else knew. Who was it?

It was the Spirit of God.

> "The anointing of THE BLESSING... empowered them to subdue and have dominion over whatever and whomever came against them."

The anointing of THE BLESSING revealed to them strategies and tactics of war no one had ever heard of before. It empowered them to subdue and have dominion over whatever and whomever came against them. The Bible doesn't tell us how God trained Abraham's servants, but they wound up knowing how to fight so effectively that a few hundred of them could rout an army of thousands. When they showed up at Ched's camp in the night, he and his troops didn't know what to do but die or run. Abraham's commandos ruled the night.

NOTES

OVERTAKEN BY THE BLESSING (VERSE 2)

DAY 3

A. All These Blessings

1. "Before the Torah recounts the dire consequences of sin, it gives the blessings that will accrue to the nation for fulfilling the commandments. These blessings are wide ranging and involve every area of material life, thus reassuring the people that their spiritual accomplishments will bring them untold benefits in every area of life." —*The Chumash, Stone Edition*

2. Psalm 103:1-5 (NKJV): "Bless the Lord, O my soul; and all that is within me, bless His holy name! Bless the Lord, O my soul, and forget not all His benefits: who forgives all your iniquities, who heals all your diseases, who redeems your life from destruction, who crowns you with lovingkindness and tender mercies, who satisfies your mouth with good things, so that your youth is renewed like the eagle's."

3. 2 Peter 1:3 (AMP): "For His divine power has bestowed upon us all things that [are requisite and suited] to life and godliness, through the [full, personal] knowledge of Him Who called us by and to His own glory and excellence (virtue)."

4. Psalm 84:11 (NKJV): "For the Lord God is a sun and shield; the Lord will give grace and glory; no good thing will He withhold from those who walk uprightly."

5. "All these blessings" include everything it will take to empower us to succeed and prosper in everything we do.

B. All These Blessings Shall Come on You and Overtake You

1. Deuteronomy 28:2 (MSG): "All these blessings will come down on you."

2. Ezekiel 34:25-27—Showers of blessing

   a. *Shower* (HEB) = to pour down and rain violently

   b. *Shower* (Merriam-Webster) = a falling of things from the air in thick succession in great and large quantities

3. Malachi 3:10: "I will...open the windows of heaven, and pour you out a blessing, that there shall not be room enough to receive it."

   a. *Brenton*—The torrents of heaven

   b. NIV—The floodgates of heaven

   c. CEV: "I will open the windows of heaven and flood you with blessing after blessing."

4. *Overtake you* (HEB) = take over your life, overwhelm you, engulf you, pile up on you, cover you over and load you up with an excessive amount, avalanche, heap, swamp, overflow, flood

5. Luke 5:6-9—Peter was overtaken with fish.

   a. Verses 6-7 (NLT): "And this time their nets were so full of fish they began to tear! A shout for help brought their partners in the other boat, and soon both boats were filled with fish and on the verge of sinking."

   b. Every fish in Galilee showed up.

   c. The sale of those fish launched Peter into his full-time ministry.

C. If You Will Hearken Unto the Voice of the Lord Thy God

1. This is the second time this statement has been made in as many verses—very important!

2. Deuteronomy 28:2 (ESV): "If you obey the voice of the Lord your God."

3. THE BLESSING is conditional to our obedience to His voice.

4. Obedience to His voice opens the door for THE BLESSING to overtake us.

5. And THE BLESSING always supplies the best.

   a. Isaiah 1:19 (NIV-84): "If you are willing and obedient, you will eat the best from the land."

   b. MSG: "If you'll willingly obey, you'll feast like kings."

> "To obey what He says, you have to know what He says and receive it."
> —Gloria Copeland

NOTES

NOTES

GLORIA COPELAND & PASTOR GEORGE PEARSONS

THE FULLNESS OF THE BLESSING (VERSES 3-6)

DAY 4

A. Galatians 3:13-14—Review of THE BLESSING

1. THE BLESSING is a declaration which empowers someone to succeed at whatever they do.

2. In Genesis 1:28, God empowered man when he was created to be fruitful, multiply, replenish the earth, subdue it and have dominion over it.

3. Man was empowered to establish the Garden of Eden wherever he went.

4. In Christ Jesus, we are to experience the fullness of THE BLESSING of Abraham.

5. Galatians 3:29 (MSG): "Also, since you are Christ's family, then you are Abraham's famous 'descendant,' heirs according to the covenant promises."
   a. Verse 7—We are children of Abraham.
   b. Verse 9—We are blessed with Abraham.

B. The Fullness of THE BLESSING

1. Deuteronomy 28:3-6 represents the fullness of THE BLESSING in every area of life.
   a. Israel has the highest rate of entrepreneurship in the world.[2]
      i. Highest among women[2] (Proverbs 31)
      ii. Highest among age 55 and above[2]
      iii. Twenty-two percent of Nobel Prize winners are Jewish[1]
   b. Israeli innovations
      i. Flash drive[3]
      ii. Cellphone[4]
      iii. Voice mail[2]

        iv.   Instant Messaging[3]

        v.   Smallest video camera (endoscope)[3]

        vi.   PillCam (digestive tract camera)[3]

        vii.   Vaccine against West Nile virus[5]

        viii. Nanowire—1,000 times thinner than human hair[3]

        ix.   Iron Dome missile defense[3]

2. Blessed in the city and in the field

    a. Wherever you are

    b. *"Blessed shalt thou be in the city*—not only in the city of Jerusalem, where the Temple would be built, and there be blessed with the service, worship, and ordinances of God, but in all other cities of the land; where they should dwell in large, and spacious houses, and their cities should be walled and fenced, and be very populous; yet should enjoy health, and have plenty of all sorts of provisions brought unto them, as well as prosper in all kinds of merchandise there, as Aben Ezra notes." —*John Gill's Exposition of the Bible*

    c. *"Blessed shalt thou be in the field*—in the country villages, and in all rural employments, in sowing and planting, as the same writer observes; in all kinds of husbandry, in the culture of the fields for corn, and of vineyards and oliveyards; all should prosper and succeed, and bring forth fruit abundantly." —*John Gill's Exposition of the Bible*

3. Blessed in the fruit of your body, your ground, your cattle, the increase of your kine and the flocks of your sheep

    a. Whatever you do

    b. *"Blessed shall be the fruit of thy body*—their children, of which they should have many, and these live; be healthful, thrive, and arrive to manhood, and increase and perpetuate their families." —*John Gill's Exposition of the Bible*

        i.   Psalm 115:14: "The Lord shall increase you more and more, you and your children."

    c. *"And the fruit of thy ground*—of their gardens, orchards, and fields; grass for the cattle, and the wheat, barley, vines, figs, pomegranates, olives, and dates for the use of men." —*John Gill's Exposition of the Bible*

    d. *"And the fruit of thy cattle, the increase of thy kine, and the flocks of thy sheep"*—simply meaning that you will be extremely productive in all you do.

        i.   Genesis 13:2 (AMP): "Abram was extremely rich in livestock and in silver and in gold."

        ii.   *Extreme*—reaching a high or the highest degree, utmost, maximum, enormous, extraordinary

4. Blessed in your basket and in your store

    a. Whatever you have

    b. A basket holds reserves, surplus, increase and overflow.

        i.   John 6:12-13—Gathered and filled 12 baskets that remained, over and above

  c. A kneading-trough is the preparation place for what is daily consumed.

    i. Matthew 6:11—Daily bread

5. Blessed when you come in and blessed when you go out

  a. Wherever you go

  b. "When you comest in from your employment, you shall find that no evil has happened to the family or dwelling in your absence." *—Adam Clarke's Commentary on the Bible*

    i. Psalm 121:8 (NKJV): "The Lord shall preserve your going out and your coming in from this time forth, and even forevermore."

  c. "When you goest out, your way shall be made prosperous before you, and you shall have the divine blessing in all your labors." *—Adam Clarke's Commentary on the Bible*

  d. "In all their business and employments of life whether within doors or without; in the administration of every office, whether more public or private; and in all their journeys going out and coming home; and particularly when they went out to war, and returned, all should be attended with success." *—John Gill's Exposition of the Bible*

C. Genesis 39:1-6—Joseph Experienced the Fullness of THE BLESSING

1. Wherever he was

2. Whatever he did

3. Whatever he had

4. Wherever he went

5. Verse 5: "THE BLESSING of the Lord was upon all that he had in the house, and in the field."

NOTES

GLORIA COPELAND & PASTOR GEORGE PEARSONS

ENEMIES ON THE RUN (VERSE 7)

DAY 5

A. Enemies Smitten Before Your Face

1. *Smitten* (HEB) = sudden, quick, decisive fatal blow with the intent to utterly conquer and destroy

2. "This is a promise of security from foreign invasion, or total discomfiture of the invaders should they enter the land." —*Adam Clarke's Commentary on the Bible*

3. 1 Samuel 17:49: "And David put his hand in his bag, and took thence a stone, and slang it, and smote the Philistine in his forehead, that the stone sunk into his forehead; and he fell upon his face to the earth."

   a. David was operating under the anointing of THE BLESSING.

   b. The confrontation ended quickly.

   c. It was a decisive fatal blow that resulted in victory.

4. Exodus 23:22 (ESV): "But if you carefully obey his voice and do all that I say, then I will be an enemy to your enemies and an adversary to your adversaries."

5. Exodus 23:27 (NLT): "I will send my terror ahead of you and create panic among all the people whose lands you invade. I will make all your enemies turn and run."

B. They Will Flee Seven Ways

1. Deuteronomy 28:7 (MSG): "God will defeat your enemies who attack you. They'll come at you on one road and run away on seven roads."

2. "It is common for people who flee in panic to disperse and run off in all directions (Rashi), discarding every semblance of military discipline. The juxtaposition of this verse with the next, which speaks of blessed storehouses, suggests that the fleeing enemy will leave behind a wealth of supplies and provisions for the Jews to take at will (Baal HaTruim)." —*The Chumash, Stone Edition*

3. "They shall come out against thee one way—in the firmest and most united manner. And flee...seven ways—shall be utterly broken, confounded, and finally routed." —*Adam Clarke's Commentary on the Bible*

4. What is so significant about the number 7?

    a. Perfection

    b. Completion

    c. Total victory

5. The seven redemptive names of God completely cover the total defeat of seven major enemies of life.

C. Seven Defeated Enemies of Life

1. The Enemy of Lack

    a. Jehovah Jireh—The Lord Will Provide

    b. Genesis 22:13-14 (NLT): "Then Abraham looked up and saw a ram caught by its horns in a thicket. So he took the ram and sacrificed it as a burnt offering in place of his son. Abraham named the place Yahweh-Yireh (which means 'the Lord will provide')."

2. The Enemy of Sickness

    a. Jehovah Rapha—The Lord That Heals

    b. Exodus 15:26 (NLT): "He said, 'If you will listen carefully to the voice of the Lord your God and do what is right in his sight, obeying his commands and keeping all his decrees, then I will not make you suffer any of the diseases I sent on the Egyptians; for I am the Lord who heals you.'"

3. The Enemy of Failure

    a. Jehovah Nissi—The Lord Our Banner and Victory

    b. Exodus 17:8-15 (NLT): "...After the victory, the Lord instructed Moses, 'Write this down on a scroll as a permanent reminder, and read it aloud to Joshua: I will erase the memory of Amalek from under heaven.' Moses built an altar there and named it Yahweh-Nissi (which means 'the Lord is my banner')."

4. The Enemy of Worry

    a. Jehovah Shalom—The Lord Our Peace

    b. Judges 6:24 (NLT): "And Gideon built an altar to the Lord there and named it Yahweh-Shalom (which means 'the Lord is peace')."

5. The Enemy of Confusion

    a. Jehovah Ra-ah—The Lord My Shepherd

    b. Psalm 23:1-3 (NKJV): "The Lord is my shepherd; I shall not want. He makes me to lie down in green pastures; He leads me beside the still waters. He restores my soul; He leads me in the paths of righteousness for His name's sake."

6. The Enemy of Condemnation

    a. Jehovah Tsidkenu—The Lord Our Righteousness

    b. Jeremiah 23:5-6 (NLT): "'For the time is coming,' says the Lord, 'when I will raise up a righteous descendant from King David's line. He will be a King who rules with wisdom. He will do what is just and right throughout the land. And this will be his name: "The Lord Is Our Righteousness." In that day Judah will be saved and Israel will live in safety.'"

7. The Enemy of Fear

    a. Jehovah Shammah—The Lord Is There

    b. Ezekiel 48:35 (NLT): "And from that day the name of the city will be 'The Lord Is There.'"

"Resist the devil, and he will flee from you [as in stark terror]."
James 4:7

NOTES

_____

_____

_____

_____

_____

_____

_____

_____

_____

_____

_____

_____

NOTES

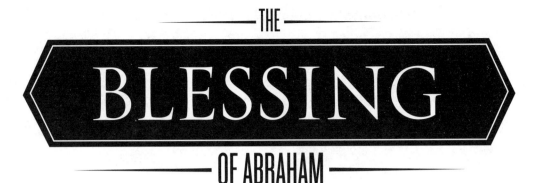

THE
BLESSING
OF ABRAHAM

GLORIA COPELAND & PASTOR GEORGE PEARSONS

THE COMMANDED BLESSING (VERSE 8)

DAY 6

A. The Lord Shall Command THE BLESSING Upon You in Your Storehouses

1. *Command* (HEB) = to give an order, charge or decree

2. THE BLESSING is a declaration which empowers someone to prosper and succeed in everything they do.

    a. Proverbs 10:22: "The blessing of the Lord, it maketh rich, and he addeth no sorrow with it."

    b. Genesis 1:28—God told Adam to be fruitful, multiply, replenish the earth, subdue it and have dominion over it.

3. *Storehouses* = multiple places where goods and wealth are stored

    a. Bank accounts, investment accounts—wherever something of value is stored

    b. God will protect and multiply whatever is in those storehouses.

    c. These storehouses were, "Barns, granaries, and cellar, where their corn, wine and oil were laid up; by preserving the corn from being devoured by vermin, and the casks of wine and oil from bursting and running out." —*John Gill's Exposition of the Bible*

4. Deuteronomy 28:8 (NLT): "The Lord will guarantee a blessing on everything you do and will fill your storehouses with grain."

5. "Everything that you have shall come by divine appointment; you shall have nothing casually, but everything, both spiritual and temporal, shall come by immediate command of God." —*Adam Clarke's Commentary on the Bible*

B. The Lord Shall Command THE BLESSING Upon All You Set Your Hand to Do

1. Everything you undertake will succeed and prosper.

   a. "In all their manufactures, occupations, and trades, in which they were employed, and in the culture of their vines, olives, and other fruit trees." —*John Gill's Exposition of the Bible*

   b. "In all thy business." —*Commentary on the Old Testament in Ten Volumes, Volume 1, The Pentateuch*

2. Deuteronomy 2:7 (NIV-84): "The Lord your God has blessed you in all the work of your hands. He has watched over your journey through this vast desert. These forty years the Lord your God has been with you, and you have not lacked anything."

3. Deuteronomy 12:7 (NIV): "There, in the presence of the Lord your God, you and your families shall eat and shall rejoice in everything you have put your hand to, because the Lord your God has blessed you."

4. Psalm 128:1-2 (NIV-84): "Blessed are all who fear the Lord, who walk in his ways. You will eat the fruit of your labor; blessings and prosperity will be yours."

5. Psalm 90:17 (NLT): "And may the Lord our God show us his approval and make our efforts successful."

C. He Shall Bless You in the Land

1. Deuteronomy 28:8 (CEV): "The Lord your God is giving you the land, and He will make sure you are successful in everything you do."

2. Deuteronomy 8:7-10—The land that God has given us

3. Genesis 26:12-13 (NLT): "When Isaac planted his crops that year, he harvested a hundred times more grain than he planted, for the Lord blessed him. He became a very rich man, and his wealth continued to grow."

   a. A hundredfold return was an unusual harvest for Gerar.

   b. Even in more fertile regions, the yield was usually not greater than twenty-five to fifty fold.

   c. Isaac's land was blessed by God in spite of a serious famine.

4. Deuteronomy 28:8: "With health and long life in it, and with an abundance of all good things, it being a land flowing with milk and honey." —*John Gill's Exposition of the Bible*

5. "God will bring the blessing of prosperity into Eretz Yisrael, so that merchants and investors will have no need to travel abroad to make their fortunes (Haamek Davar)." —*The Chumash, Stone Edition*

"What is blessed can't be cursed."
—Gloria Copeland

NOTES

NOTES

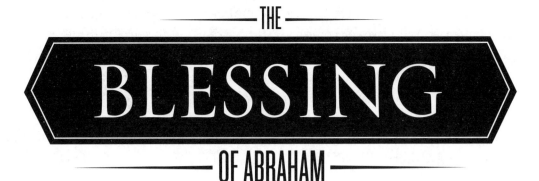

GLORIA COPELAND & PASTOR GEORGE PEARSONS

THE BLESSING CLEARLY SEEN (VERSES 9-10)

DAY 7

A. A Holy People for God

1. *Establish* (HEB) = raised up to become a powerful people; to bring them on the scene

2. *Holy* (HEB) = set apart, consecrated, purified, protected from ruin

3. Holy people = blessed people

4. THE BLESSING sets us apart to bring us on the scene and be a powerful people.

5. Deuteronomy 26:19 (NIV): "He has declared that he will set you in praise, fame and honor high above all the nations he has made and that you will be a people holy to the Lord your God, as he promised."

6. 1 Peter 2:9 (NIV-84): "But you are a chosen people, a royal priesthood, a holy nation, a people belonging to God, that you may declare the praises of him who called you out of darkness into his wonderful light."

B. People Will See You Are Called by God

1. What about us will they see?

2. Deuteronomy 28:10—They will see we are "called his children, his people, his portion, and his inheritance; and that they are his, and he is theirs, by the care he takes of them, the provision he makes for them, and the protection they have from him." —*John Gill's Exposition of the Bible*

3. Genesis 26:26-29 (NLT): "One day King Abimelech came from Gerar with his adviser, Ahuzzath, and also Phicol, his army commander. 'Why have you come here?' Isaac asked. 'You obviously hate me, since you kicked me off your land.' They replied, 'We can plainly see that the Lord is with you. So we want to enter into a sworn treaty with you. Let's make a covenant. Swear that you will not harm us, just as we have never troubled you. We have always treated you well, and we sent you away from us in peace. And now look how the Lord has blessed you!'"

4. They will see that we are prospering, enlarging, increasing and walking in the overwhelming abundance of God in every realm of life.

5. Deuteronomy 28:10 (NLT): "Then all the nations of the world will see that you are a people claimed by the Lord."

6. "They will see your blessing and prosperity. Your blessing is a sign. You shall be a testimony." —Gloria Copeland

C. People Will Be Astonished

1. The God they see in us will cause a reaction in them.

2. *Awe* (HEB) = reverence, fear, honor, respect

   a. To inspire godly fear

   b. To cause astonishment

   c. In other words, "Don't mess with My people!"

3. Deuteronomy 28:10 (MSG): "All the peoples on Earth will see you living under the Name of God and hold you in respectful awe."

4. "In the plain sense of the verse, it will be natural for nations to feel reverence for a people that is such an obvious recipient of God's blessings, for this Divine bounty will testify to the Name that they bear upon themselves. Each nation will have its god or set of beliefs, but all nations will come to realize that only God is the source of all strength and blessing—even of the powers that they ascribe to their gods. If so, the nation that is intimately associated with God will inspire the awe of all the others (R' Bachya)." —*The Chumash, Stone Edition*

5. 2 Chronicles 9:3-4 (NLT): "When the queen of Sheba realized how wise Solomon was, and when she saw the palace he had built, she was overwhelmed. She was also amazed at the food on his tables, the organization of his officials and their splendid clothing, the cup-bearers and their robes, and the burnt offerings Solomon made at the Temple of the Lord."

6. Deuteronomy 11:24-25 (NLT): "Wherever you set foot, that land will be yours. Your frontiers will stretch from the wilderness in the south to Lebanon in the north, and from the Euphrates River in the east to the Mediterranean Sea in the west. No one will be able to stand against you, for the Lord your God will cause the people to fear and dread you, as he promised, wherever you go in the whole land."

7. Isaiah 61:9 (NIV): "Their descendants will be known among the nations and their offspring among the peoples. All who see them will acknowledge that they are a people the Lord has blessed."

NOTES

NOTES

THE BLESSING OF ABRAHAM

GLORIA COPELAND & PASTOR GEORGE PEARSONS

A SURPLUS OF PROSPERITY (VERSE 11)

DAY 8

A. The Lord Shall Make You Plenteous in Goods

1. We were created by God to be fully supplied in every possible way.

2. You have plenty of everything.

3. Proverbs 10:22: "The blessing of the Lord, it maketh rich, and he addeth no sorrow with it."

4. *Plenteous* (HEB) = abundance, to have more than enough, to have excess, too much with much left over

5. *Plenteous* = plenty of everything

6. *Goods* (HEB) = prosperity, wealth, good things, beautiful things, the best things

7. God enjoys prospering His people.

   a. Deuteronomy 30:9 (ESV): "The Lord your God will make you abundantly prosperous in all the work of your hand, in the fruit of your womb and in the fruit of your cattle and in the fruit of your ground. For the Lord will again take delight in prospering you, as he took delight in your fathers."

   b. Psalm 35:27: "Let them shout for joy, and be glad, that favour my righteous cause: yea, let them say continually, Let the Lord be magnified, which hath pleasure in the prosperity of his servant."

B. A Surplus of Prosperity

1. Deuteronomy 28: 11 (AMP): "And the Lord shall make you have a surplus of prosperity."

   a. *Surplus* (Merriam-Webster) = an amount that is more than the amount needed

   b. VOICE: "The Eternal will give you more than enough of every good thing."

      c.   Exodus 36:7 (NLT): "Their contributions were more than enough to complete the whole project."

      d.   "Where does the surplus come from? It comes from THE BLESSING working on your behalf. It works and it works and it works, and it keeps working!"—Gloria Copeland

2.   MSG: "God will lavish you with good things."

      a.   *Lavish* (The Free Dictionary) = to expend or give in great amounts or without limit

      b.   1 John 3:1 (NIV-84): "How great is the love the Father has lavished on us, that we should be called the children of God!"

3.   BBE: "The Lord will make you fertile in every good thing."

      a.   *Fertile* (Merriam-Webster) = producing a large amount of something

      b.   Genesis 26:12-14 (NIV): "Isaac planted crops in that land and the same year reaped a hundredfold, because the Lord blessed him. The man became rich, and his wealth continued to grow until he became very wealthy. He had so many flocks and herds and servants that the Philistines envied him."

4.   EXB: "The Lord will make you rich."

5.   "Superabundance will the Lord give thee for good (for happiness and prosperity)." —*Commentary on the Old Testament in Ten Volumes, Volume 1, The Pentateuch*

      a.   *Superabundant* (Dictionary.com) = exceedingly or excessively abundant; more than sufficient

      b.   Ephesians 3:20 (AMP): "Now to Him Who, by (in consequence of) the [action of His] power that is at work within us, is able to [carry out His purpose and] do superabundantly, far over and above all that we [dare] ask or think [infinitely beyond our highest prayers, desires, thoughts, hopes, or dreams]."

C. THE BLESSING Produces Fruit

1.   Fruit—the result of listening to God's voice, walking in God's ways and following God's commands

2.   Deuteronomy 28:11 (MSG): "God will lavish you with good things: children from your womb, offspring from your animals, and crops from your land, the land that God promised your ancestors that he would give you."

3.   NLT: "The Lord will give you prosperity in the land he swore to your ancestors to give you, blessing you with many children, numerous livestock, and abundant crops."

4.   The fruit of your ground is your sowing and reaping.

5.   This was an irreversible covenant oath that God promised to Abraham.

NOTES

NOTES

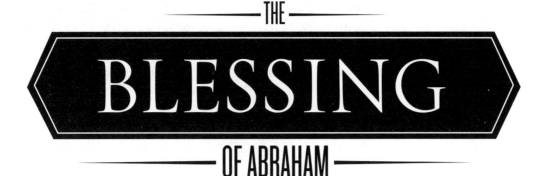

THE BLESSING OF ABRAHAM

GLORIA COPELAND & PASTOR GEORGE PEARSONS

TREASURES FROM HEAVEN (VERSE 12)

DAY 9

A. The Lord Will Open His Good Treasure

1. *Open* (HEB) = throw wide open and let loose

2. *Treasure* (HEB) = storehouse, armory, depository, treasury

    a. BBE: "Opening his store-house in heaven."

    b. CEV: "The Lord will open the storehouses of the skies."

    c. NIV: "The Lord will open the heavens, the storehouse of his bounty."

    d. CEB: "The Lord will open up for you his own well-stocked storehouse."

    e. MSG: "God will throw open the doors of his sky vaults."

B. Words From the Lord Through Kenneth Copeland Regarding God's Storehouse

1. "'...I have a great storehouse. Much more has been stored up in the storehouse of riches beyond your wildest dream that I laid up for you before the foundation of the world. Much more is stored up there than what the Church has ever called for. I never have held back on the Church,' saith The Lord, the God of plenty. 'I've made it available to you. I put it in My WORD. I gave you a promise and stood behind it with the blood—the precious blood of your Savior. But there has been a backwardness in My people about laying hold of the things that I have provided for you. But I will say this: There is a people in the land. There is a people around the world. There is a people strong and mighty, growing much stronger and much mightier and more bold to lay hold and put their claim of faith on the things that I have laid up for you and it thrills Me,' saith The Lord, 'because it's been yours all the time.'" —"God's Great Storehouse" word from the Lord through Kenneth Copeland, Nov. 10, 2011

2. "'I have plans that you have never dreamed of,' saith The LORD. 'They are beyond your wildest imagination. I did it just for you. Heaven is overloaded with things that I have prepared for your enjoyment, if you will simply come to that place where you just say, "God, I am so grateful," and give Me an opportunity.'" —"Come to the Table," word from the Lord through Kenneth Copeland, Aug. 7, 2009

3. "God is The LORD of the storehouse. He is the treasurer.... He's The LORD of the harvest. He's The LORD of the treasure. He's The LORD of the treasure house, which is part of THE BLESSING of Abraham in Deuteronomy 28:12. That is part of what will come on us and overtake us, if we hearken to the commandment of The LORD."—"The Lord of the Storehouse," word from the Lord through Kenneth Copeland, Jan. 23, 2012

C. He Will Give Rain for Your Land

1. Deuteronomy 28:12 (MSG): "God will throw open the doors of his sky vaults and pour rain on your land on schedule and bless the work you take in hand."

2. Leviticus 26:3-5 (MSG): "If you live by my decrees and obediently keep my commandments, I will send the rains in their seasons, the ground will yield its crops and the trees of the field their fruit. You will thresh until the grape harvest and the grape harvest will continue until planting time."

    a. Leviticus 26:10 (NLT-96): "You will have such a surplus of crops that you will need to get rid of the leftovers from the previous year to make room for each new harvest."

3. Isaiah 30:23 (NIV): "He will also send you rain for the seed you sow in the ground, and the food that comes from the land will be rich and plentiful."

D. He Will Bless the Work of Your Hands

1. *Work* (HEB) = labor, business, pursuit, undertaking, enterprise, occupation, transactions, endeavors

2. Deuteronomy 30:9 (NLT): "The Lord your God will then make you successful in everything you do."

    a. Genesis 39:3 (NIV): "When his master saw that the Lord was with him and that the Lord gave him success in everything he did." (Joseph)

    b. 1 Samuel 18:14 (NIV): "In everything he did he had great success, because the Lord was with him." (David)

    c. The more you obey God's Word (the more you get in the Word and see what God says), and you make changes to agree with what God tells you to do, the greater THE BLESSING is going to flow.

    d. "Whatever comes out of your mouth, comes out of the abundance of your heart unless it is just something you mentally decide to do. What you continually say, is what you're going to get." —Gloria Copeland

3. Psalm 1:1-3 (NKJV): "Blessed is the man who walks not in the counsel of the ungodly, nor stands in the path of sinners, nor sits in the seat of the scornful; but his delight is in the law of the Lord, and in His law he meditates day and night. He shall be like a tree planted by the rivers of water, that brings forth its fruit in its season, whose leaf also shall not wither; and whatever he does shall prosper."

E. You Will Lend and Not Borrow

1. Deuteronomy 28:12 (NLT): "You will lend to many nations, but you will never need to borrow from them."

2. MSG: "God will throw open the doors of His sky vaults and pour rain on your land on schedule and bless the work you take in hand. You will lend to many nations but you yourself won't have to take out a loan."

3. "The manifestation of THE BLESSING is at an all-time high. You are approaching a blessing manifestation of Glory that is an explosion in ways and intensity that the human race has never seen before.... THE BLESSING will encase you and you will learn to walk in the secret place of the Most High God. Blessed in His BLESSING, blessed in His Glory, blessed in your comings, blessed in your goings. Blessed in your pocketbook. All debt will have to get up and leave you the way leprosy left the lepers of old. Debt is financial sickness. It is financial leprosy. It is an attempt to do with the natural world's monies and abilities what I created THE BLESSING to do for you. Only, it is a burden and not a blessing. Debt is part of the curse. If you will begin to confess [the Word], you will be shocked and thrilled at how quickly you will have the Glory arise and drive the debt out of your life. If you will bring your tithe to Me and spend time with Me, tithing that tithe to Me, I will teach you, and I will train you, and I will show you how to be debt free. I will bless you beyond your means. I will bless you beyond your income. I will bless you beyond your salaries. I will bless you beyond anything you have ever known before...." —"And I Will Bless You Beyond Your Means" word from the Lord through Kenneth Copeland, July 9, 2007

4. Romans 13:8 (AMP): "Keep out of debt!"

5. The moment you make the quality decision to live debt free, God sees you debt free!

> "A decision to be debt free takes you from what you can afford to what you desire.
> It takes the limits off."
> —Gloria Copeland

NOTES

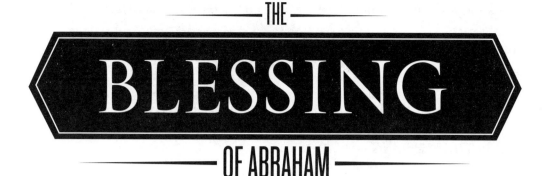

GLORIA COPELAND & PASTOR GEORGE PEARSONS

THE HEAD AND NOT THE TAIL (VERSES 13-14)

DAY 10

A. The Head and Not the Tail—Above and Not Beneath

1. *Head* (HEB) = top, summit, upper part, chief, leader, captain

2. *Tail* (HEB) = end, stump, attacked in the rear, flapping

3. Deuteronomy 28:13 (NIV): "You will always be at the top, never at the bottom."

4. ESV: "You shall only go up and not down."

5. "Thou wilt rise more and more, and increase in wealth, power and dignity." —*Commentary on the Old Testament in Ten Volumes, Volume 1, The Pentateuch*

B. The Borrower Is a Slave to the Lender

1. Note the connection between Deuteronomy 28:12 and 28:13.
   a. Verse 12: "Thou shalt lend unto many nations, and thou shalt not borrow."
   b. Verse 13: "The Lord shall make thee the head and not the tail; and thou shalt be above only, and thou shalt not be beneath."

2. Proverbs 22:7 (ESV): "The rich rules over the poor, and the borrower is the slave of the lender."

3. The borrower becomes the tail and ends up subservient to the lender.

4. Deuteronomy 15:4-6 (NLT): "There should be no poor among you, for the Lord your God will greatly bless you in the land he is giving you as a special possession. You will receive this blessing if you are careful to obey all the commands of the Lord your God that I am giving you today. The Lord your God will bless you as he has promised. You will lend money to many nations but will never need to borrow. You will rule many nations, but they will not rule over you."

5. "God's blessing will eliminate poverty and the need for loans." —*The Chumash, Stone Edition*

6. Proverbs 22:7 (MSG): "The poor are always ruled over by the rich, so don't borrow and put yourself under their power."

7. The moment you make the quality decision to become debt free, God sees you debt free.

C. Keep Your Eyes on THE BLESSING

1. Deuteronomy 28:14 (MSG): "Don't swerve an inch to the right or left from the words that I command you today by going off following and worshiping other gods."

2. "You don't need other gods when you have Me!"
   a. "I will provide everything you need."
   b. "I will get you out of debt."
   c. "I will help you live debt free."

3. Joshua 1:7 (NIV): "Be strong and very courageous. Be careful to obey all the law my servant Moses gave you; do not turn from it to the right or to the left, that you may be successful wherever you go."

"Fear stops you at the gate of abundance. Faith keeps the gate of abundance wide open."
—Gloria Copeland

NOTES

NOTES